Section 1

Contents

TEST 1	Adding and subtracting 1
TEST 2	Adding and subtracting 2
TEST 3	Adding and subtracting 10
TEST 4	Number pairs that make 10
TEST 5	Adding and subtracting 9
TEST 6	Adding and subtracting 8
TEST 7	Doubles
TEST 8	**Near doubles** (a number pair where one number is 1 more than the other)
TEST 9	**Near near doubles** (a number pair where one number is 2 more than the other)
TEST 10	Sets of 2
TEST 11	A mixture of tests 1 to 9 to test progress
TEST 12	A mixture of tests 1 to 10 to test progress

Date started:

Date finished:

Achievement Chart for Section 1
Colour the appropriate box for each question you got right

		1	2	3	4	5	6	7	8	9	10
Test 1	Part A										
	Part B										
	Part C										
Test 2	Part A										
	Part B										
	Part C										
Test 3	Part A										
	Part B										
	Part C										
Test 4	Part A										
	Part B										
	Part C										
Test 5	Part A										
	Part B										
	Part C										
Test 6	Part A										
	Part B										
	Part C										
Test 7	Part A										
	Part B										
	Part C										
Test 8	Part A										
	Part B										
	Part C										
Test 9	Part A										
	Part B										
	Part C										
Test 10	Part A										
	Part B										
	Part C										
Test 11	Part A										
	Part B										
	Part C										
Test 12	Part A										
	Part B										
	Part C										

Section 1   Test 1

A		ANSWER
1		
2		
3	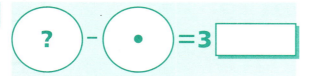	
4		
5		
6		
7	 Write the name of this shape.	
8	Which pencil is longer? 	
9	Which day comes after Tuesday?	
10	 What time is it? _____ o'clock	

B	✓	ANSWER
1	4 + 1 =	
2	14 + 1 =	
3	24 + 1 =	
4	14, 15, 16, 17, ▢	
5	7 − 1 =	
6	17 − 1 =	
7	27 − 1 =	
8	27, 26, 25, 24, ▢	
9	▢ + 1 = 4	
10	▢ − 1 = 8	

C		ANSWER
1	Add 7 and 1. ✓	
2	Take 1 from 5.	
3	The total of 8 and 1 is	
4	The difference between 1 and 6 is	
5	The sum of 1 and 9 is	
6	3 is 1 more than	
7	Subtract 1 from 9.	
8	4 minus 1 is	
9	1 less than 8 is	
10	1 plus 6 is	

Section 1 Test 2

A		ANSWER
1		
2		
3		
4		p
5		p
6		p
7	 Write the name of this shape.	
8	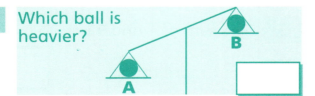 Which ball is heavier?	
9	Which day comes before Saturday?	
10	What time is it?	o'clock

B	✓	ANSWER
1	6 + 2 =	
2	16 + 2 =	
3	26 + 2 =	
4	16, 18, 20, 22, ☐	
5	5 − 2 =	
6	15 − 2 =	
7	25 − 2 =	
8	25, 23, 21, 19, ☐	
9	☐ + 2 = 4	
10	☐ − 2 = 8	

C	✓	ANSWER
1	Add 8 and 2.	
2	Take 2 from 9.	
3	The total of 6 and 2 is	
4	The difference between 2 and 8 is	
5	The sum of 2 and 9 is	
6	4 is 2 more than	
7	Subtract 2 from 5.	
8	3 minus 2 is	
9	2 less than 6 is	
10	2 plus 7 is	

Section 1 Test 3

A		ANSWER
1		
2		
3	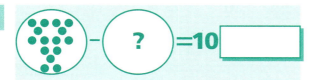	
4		p
5		p
6		p
7	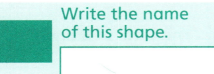 Write the name of this shape.	
8	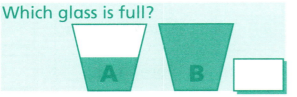 Which glass is full?	
9	Which day comes after Monday?	
10	 What time is it?	o'clock

B		ANSWER
1	3 + 10 =	
2	13 + 10 =	
3	23 + 10 =	
4	13, 23, 33, 43, ▪	
5	11 – 10 =	
6	21 – 10 =	
7	31 – 10 =	
8	51, 41, 31, 21, ▪	
9	▪ + 10 = 46	
10	▪ – 10 = 27	

C		ANSWER
1	Add 10 and 3.	
2	Take 10 from 19.	
3	The total of 10 and 5 is	
4	The difference between 15 and 10 is	
5	The sum of 10 and 6 is	
6	12 is 10 more than	
7	Subtract 10 from 18.	
8	11 minus 10 is	
9	10 is 4 less than	
10	10 plus 7 is	

Section 1 Test 4

A		ANSWER
1		
2		
3		
4	 p	
5	 p	
6		
7	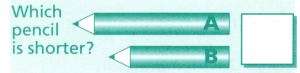 Write the name of this shape.	
8	Which pencil is shorter?	
9	Which day comes before Friday?	
10	 What time is it? _____ o'clock	

B		ANSWER
1	6 + 4 =	
2	16 + 4 =	
3	46 + 4 =	
4	26, 36, 46, 56, ▪	
5	10 − 3 =	
6	20 − 3 =	
7	30 − 3 =	
8	67, 57, 47, 37, ▪	
9	▪ + 5 = 10	
10	10 − ▪ = 9	

C		ANSWER
1	Add 3 and 7.	
2	Take 9 from 10.	
3	The total of 8 and 2 is	
4	The difference between 5 and 10 is	
5	The sum of 4 and 6 is	
6	10 is 3 more than	
7	Subtract 8 from 10.	
8	10 minus 1 is	
9	6 is 4 less than	
10	2 plus 8 is	

Section 1 Test 5

A ANSWER

1.
2.
3.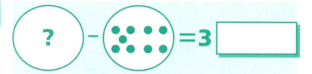
4.  p
5.  p
6.  p
7. Write the name of this shape.
8. Which ball is lighter?
9. Which day comes after Sunday?
10. What time is it? o'clock

B ANSWER

1. 7 + 9 =
2. 17 + 9 =
3. 27 + 9 =
4. 9, 18, 27, 36, ☐
5. 14 − 9 =
6. 24 − 9 =
7. 44 − 9 =
8. 54, 45, 36, 27, ☐
9. ☐ + 9 = 15
10. 12 − ☐ = 9

C ANSWER

1. Add 4 and 9.
2. Take 9 from 14.
3. The total of 9 and 5 is
4. The difference between 12 and 9 is
5. The sum of 9 and 8 is
6. 12 is 9 more than
7. Subtract 9 from 13.
8. 15 minus 9 is
9. 9 is 7 less than
10. 9 plus 3 is

Section 1 Test 6

A ANSWER

1.
2.
3.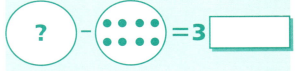
4.  p
5.  p
6. 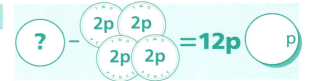 p
7.  Write the name of this shape.
8. Which person is taller? A B
9. Which day comes before Thursday?
10. What time is it? o'clock

B ANSWER

1. $5 + 8 =$
2. $15 + 8 =$
3. $35 + 8 =$
4. 8, 16, 24, 32, ▇
5. $14 - 8 =$
6. $24 - 8 =$
7. $44 - 8 =$
8. 48, 40, 32, 24, ▇
9. ▇ $+ 8 = 15$
10. $12 -$ ▇ $= 8$

C ANSWER

1. Add 7 and 8.
2. Take 8 from 14.
3. The total of 8 and 4 is
4. The difference between 15 and 8 is
5. The sum of 8 and 3 is
6. 12 is 8 more than
7. Subtract 8 from 13.
8. 11 minus 8 is
9. 8 is 5 less than
10. 8 plus 6 is

Section 1 Test 7

A		ANSWER
1		
2		
3		
4		p
5		p
6		p
7	How much is shaded? 	
8	Which glass is half full?	
9	If today is Monday, what was yesterday?	
10	 What time is it?	o'clock

B		ANSWER
1	6 + 6 =	
2	16 + 6 =	
3	26 + 6 =	
4	1, 2, 4, 8, ▢	
5	16 − 8 =	
6	26 − 8 =	
7	36 − 8 =	
8	16, 8, 4, 2, ▢	
9	▢ + 9 = 18	
10	▢ − 7 = 7	

C		ANSWER
1	Add 8 and 8.	
2	Take 7 from 14.	
3	The total of 5 and 5 is	
4	The difference between 18 and 9 is	
5	The sum of 6 and 6 is	
6	8 is 4 more than	
7	Subtract 5 from 10.	
8	6 minus 3 is	
9	7 is 7 less than	
10	9 plus 9 is	

Section 1 Test 8

A | ANSWER

1.
2.
3.  = 4
4.  p
5.  p
6.  = 6p p
7.  How much is shaded?
8. 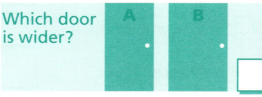 Which door is wider?
9. If today is Wednesday, what was yesterday?
10. What time is it? _____ o'clock

B | ANSWER

1. 3 + 4 =
2. 13 + 4 =
3. 53 + 4 =
4. 3, 7, 11, 15, ▢
5. 9 − 4 =
6. 19 − 4 =
7. 39 − 4 =
8. 29, 25, 21, 17, ▢
9. ▢ + 5 = 11
10. ▢ − 7 = 8

C | ANSWER

1. Add 6 and 7.
2. Take 9 from 19.
3. The total of 6 and 5 is
4. The difference between 5 and 9 is
5. The sum of 4 and 3 is
6. 5 is 2 more than
7. Subtract 7 from 15.
8. 17 minus 8 is
9. 5 is 6 less than
10. 8 plus 7 is

Section 1 Test 9

A		ANSWER
1		
2		
3		
4		p
5		p
6		p
7	 How much is shaded?	
8	How much longer is **A** than **B**? A _____ 14 cm B ____ 6 cm	cm
9	If today is Friday, what will tomorrow be?	
10	 What time is it?	o'clock

B		ANSWER
1	5 + 3 =	
2	15 + 3 =	
3	35 + 3 =	
4	5, 8, 11, 14, ☐	
5	7 − 5 =	
6	17 − 5 =	
7	57 − 5 =	
8	37, 32, 27, 22, ☐	
9	☐ + 5 = 8	
10	☐ − 7 = 5	

C		ANSWER
1	Add 6 and 8.	
2	Take 9 from 15.	
3	The total of 3 and 5 is	
4	The difference between 5 and 12 is	
5	The sum of 4 and 6 is	
6	6 is 2 more than	
7	Subtract 7 from 12.	
8	18 minus 8 is	
9	1 is 3 less than	
10	9 plus 7 is	

Section 1   Test 10

A

1. Turn the picture into a sum. ___ sets of ___
2. Turn the picture into a sum. ___ sets of ___
3. ●● × 6 =
4. ●●●●●●●● ÷ 2 =
5. 2p 2p 2p 2p How much altogether? ___ p
6. 2p × ☐ = 10p
7. 20p ÷ 2 = ___ p
8. B is twice as heavy as A. How heavy is B? A=10 g ___ g
9. If today is Sunday, what was yesterday?
10. What time is it? ___ o'clock

B

1. 2, 4, 6, 8, ☐
2. 2 + 2 + 2 =
3. 3 × 2 =
4. 2+2+2+2+2+2+2=
5. 7 × 2 =
6. 20, 18, 16, ☐, 12
7. 6 − 2 − 2 − 2 =
8. 6 ÷ 2 =
9. 14 ÷ 2 =
10. 12 ÷ 2 =

C

1. 8 sets of 2 are
2. How many twos in 10?
3. 4 twos are
4. How many 2p coins make 20p?
5. 9 times 2 is
6. 6 multiplied by 2 is
7. 8 shared among 2 is
8. Half of 18 is
9. 6 divided by 2 is
10. How many socks are there in 10 pairs?

Section 1   Test 11

A — ANSWER

1.
2.
3.
4.  p
5.  p
6.  p
7. Which shape is cut in half?
8. 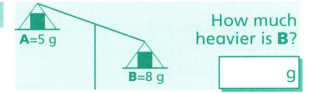 How much heavier is **B**? ___ g
9. If today is Thursday, what will tomorrow be?
10.  What time is it? ___ o'clock

B — ANSWER

1. 6 + 7 =
2. 46 + 7 =
3. 3 + 9 =
4. 73 + 9 =
5. 1, 3, 5, 7, ▢
6. 18 − 9 =
7. 38 − 9 =
8. 17 − 10 =
9. 57 − 10 =
10. 19, 17, 15, 13, ▢

C — ANSWER

1. Add 5 and 8.
2. Take 6 from 11.
3. The total of 6 and 8 is
4. The difference between 13 and 4 is
5. The sum of 7 and 5 is
6. 16 is 9 more than
7. Subtract 3 from 7.
8. 17 minus 9 is
9. 5 is 3 less than
10. 7 plus 7 is

Section 1 Test 12

A

1.  × 2 =
2. 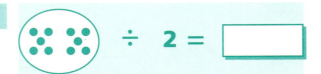 ÷ 2 =
3.  − ? = 7
4.  = ___ p
5.  = ___ p
6.  − ? = 5p
7. Which shape is cut into quarters? A  B C
8. A is twice as long as B. How long is A?
   B = 4 cm ___ cm
9. If today is Saturday, what will tomorrow be?
10. What time is it? ___ o'clock

B

1. 8 + 4 =
2. 38 + 4 =
3. 9 − 6 =
4. 29 − 6 =
5. ▨ + 4 = 10
6. ▨ − 9 = 8
7. 4, 6, 8, 10, ▨
8. 6 × 2 =
9. 16, 14, 12, 10, ▨
10. 18 ÷ 2 =

C

1. 9 sets of 2 are
2. How many twos in 14?
3. The total of 5 and 9 is
4. The difference between 6 and 15 is
5. The sum of 4 and 8 is
6. 9 is 4 more than
7. Subtract 7 from 16.
8. 12 shared among 2 is
9. 9 is 4 less than
10. 8 multiplied by 2 is

Section 2

Contents

TEST 1	Adding and subtracting, making 11
TEST 2	Adding and subtracting, making 12
TEST 3	Adding and subtracting, making 13
TEST 4	Adding and subtracting, making 14
TEST 5	Adding and subtracting, making 15
TEST 6	Adding and subtracting, making 16
TEST 7	Adding and subtracting, making 17
TEST 8	Adding and subtracting, making 18
TEST 9	Adding and subtracting, making 19
TEST 10	Sets of 10
TEST 11	A mixture of tests 1 to 9 to test progress
TEST 12	A mixture of tests 1 to 10 to test progress

Date started:

Date finished:

Achievement Chart for Section 2

Colour the appropriate box for each question you got right

		1	2	3	4	5	6	7	8	9	10
Test 1	Part A										
	Part B										
	Part C										
Test 2	Part A										
	Part B										
	Part C										
Test 3	Part A										
	Part B										
	Part C										
Test 4	Part A										
	Part B										
	Part C										
Test 5	Part A										
	Part B										
	Part C										
Test 6	Part A										
	Part B										
	Part C										
Test 7	Part A										
	Part B										
	Part C										
Test 8	Part A										
	Part B										
	Part C										
Test 9	Part A										
	Part B										
	Part C										
Test 10	Part A										
	Part B										
	Part C										
Test 11	Part A										
	Part B										
	Part C										
Test 12	Part A										
	Part B										
	Part C										

Section 2   Test 1

A

1.  How many sticks?

2.  Write the number of cubes in words.

3. Draw beads on the abacus to show the number eleven.
 tens   units

4. The total value of the coins is 11p. Which coin is missing?
 5p 5p ?   ___ p

5. How much more do you need to make 20p?
 10p 1p   ___ p

6. You have 1p 10p   You spend 5p
 How much have you got left? ___ p

7. You have 11p   You buy 9p
 How much change do you get? ___ p

8. You have 1p 5p 5p   You win 5p
 How much do you have now? ___ p

9. Which month comes after March?

10. 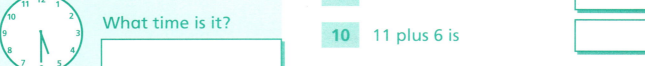 What time is it?

B

1. 6 + 10 + 1 =
2. 16 + 10 + 1 =
3. 26 + 10 + 1 =
4. 36 + 11 =
5. 24 + 11 =
6. 17 − 10 − 1 =
7. 27 − 10 − 1 =
8. 37 − 11 =
9. ☐ − 11 = 46
10. ☐ + 11 = 45

C

1. Add 7 and 11.
2. Take 5 from 11.
3. The total of 8 and 11 is
4. The difference between 11 and 6 is
5. The sum of 11 and 9 is
6. 11 is 7 more than
7. Subtract 9 from 11.
8. 11 minus 4 is
9. 8 less than 11 is
10. 11 plus 6 is

19

Section 2 Test 2

A | ANSWER

1. How many sticks?

2. Write the number of cubes in words.

3. Draw beads on the abacus to show the number twelve.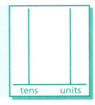

4. The total value of the coins is 12p. Which coin is missing? 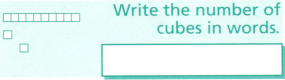 ___ p

5. How much more do you need to make 20p? 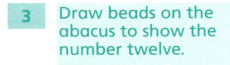 ___ p

6. You have 2p 10p You spend 5p. How much have you got left? ___ p

7. You have 12p You buy 9p. How much change do you get? ___ p

8. You have 2p You win 5p 5p 5p. How much do you have now? ___ p

9. Which month comes before June?

10.  What time is it?

B | ANSWER

1. 5 + 10 + 2 =
2. 15 + 10 + 2 =
3. 25 + 10 + 2 =
4. 35 + 12 =
5. 26 + 12 =
6. 19 − 10 − 2 =
7. 29 − 10 − 2 =
8. 39 − 12 =
9. ■ − 12 = 49
10. ■ + 12 = 47

C | ANSWER

1. Add 14 and 12.
2. Take 7 from 12.
3. The total of 9 and 12 is
4. The difference between 12 and 8 is
5. The sum of 12 and 6 is
6. 12 is 4 more than
7. Subtract 3 from 12.
8. 12 minus 5 is
9. 10 less than 12 is
10. 12 plus 7 is

20

Section 2   Test 3

A | ANSWER

1. 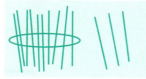 How many sticks?

2. Write the number of cubes in words.

3. Draw beads on the abacus to show the number thirteen.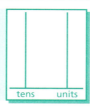

4. The total value of the coins is 13p. Which coin is missing?   ___ p

5. How much more do you need to make 20p?   ___ p

6. You have You spend
   How much have you got left? ___ p

7. You have  You buy
   How much change do you get? ___ p

8. You have  You find
   How much do you have now? ___ p

9. Which month comes before January?

10. What time is it?

B | ANSWER

1. 4 + 10 + 3 =
2. 14 + 10 + 3 =
3. 24 + 13 =
4. 34 + 13 =
5. 25 + 13 =
6. 17 − 10 − 3 =
7. 27 − 10 − 3 =
8. 37 − 13 =
9. ☐ − 13 = 43
10. ☐ + 13 = 47

C | ANSWER

1. Add 6 and 13.
2. Take 4 from 13.
3. The total of 5 and 13 is
4. The difference between 13 and 8 is
5. The sum of 13 and 7 is
6. 13 is 7 more than
7. Subtract 4 from 13.
8. 13 minus 3 is
9. 9 less than 13 is
10. 13 plus 10 is

Section 2 Test 4

A

1.  How many sticks?

2. Write the number of cubes in words.

3. Draw beads on the abacus to show the number fourteen.

4. The total value of the coins is 14p. Which coin is missing?  p

5. How much more do you need to make 20p?  p

6. You have You lose How much have you got left? p

7. You have 14p You buy 9p  How much change do you get? p

8. You have You find How much do you have now? p

9. Which month comes after September?

10.  What time is it?

B

1. 6 + 10 + 4 =
2. 16 + 14 =
3. 26 + 14 =
4. 36 + 14 =
5. 56 + 14 =
6. 19 − 10 − 4 =
7. 29 − 10 − 4 =
8. 39 − 14 =
9. ▇ − 14 = 45
10. ▇ + 14 = 40

C

1. Add 5 and 14.
2. Take 5 from 14.
3. The total of 6 and 14 is
4. The difference between 14 and 6 is
5. The sum of 14 and 9 is
6. 14 is 7 more than
7. Subtract 9 from 14.
8. 14 minus 4 is
9. 8 less than 14 is
10. 14 plus 3 is

22

Section 2   Test 5

A | ANSWER

1. 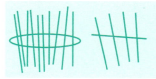 How many sticks?

2. Write the number of cubes in words.

3. Draw beads on the abacus to show the number fifteen.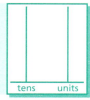

4. The total value of the coins is 15p. Which coin is missing?  ___ p

5. How much more do you need to make 20p? ___ p

6. You have You lose
How much have you got left? ___ p

7. You have 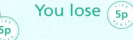 You buy
How much change do you get? ___ p

8. You have 10p 5p You find 5p
How much do you have now? ___ p

9. Which month comes after July?

10.  What time is it?

B | ANSWER

1. 5 + 10 + 5 =
2. 15 + 15 =
3. 25 + 15 =
4. 35 + 15 =
5. 55 + 15 =
6. 15 − 10 − 5 =
7. 25 − 15 =
8. 35 − 15 =
9. ▇ − 15 = 45
10. ▇ + 15 = 60

C | ANSWER

1. Add 10 and 15.
2. Take 7 from 15.
3. The total of 3 and 15 is
4. The difference between 15 and 6 is
5. The sum of 15 and 9 is
6. 15 is 5 more than
7. Subtract 9 from 15.
8. 15 minus 8 is
9. 4 less than 15 is
10. 15 plus 6 is

Section 2 Test 6

A

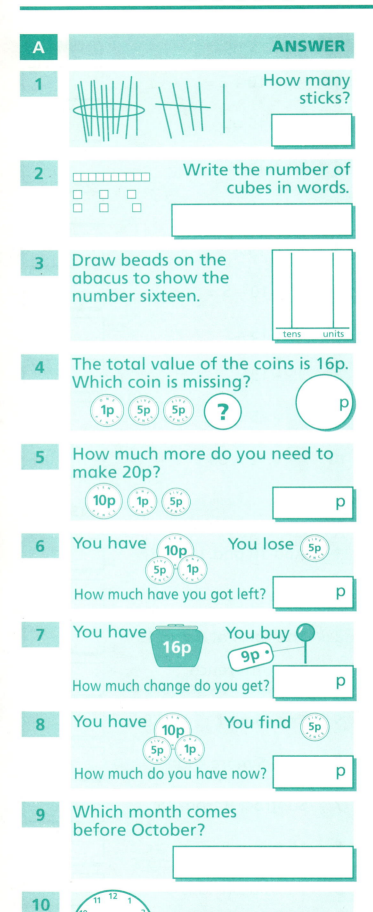

1. How many sticks?

2. Write the number of cubes in words.

3. Draw beads on the abacus to show the number sixteen.

4. The total value of the coins is 16p. Which coin is missing? 1p 5p 5p ? ___ p

5. How much more do you need to make 20p? 10p 1p 5p ___ p

6. You have 10p 5p 1p. You lose 5p. How much have you got left? ___ p

7. You have 16p. You buy 9p. How much change do you get? ___ p

8. You have 10p 5p 1p. You find 5p. How much do you have now? ___ p

9. Which month comes before October?

10. What time is it?

B

1. 2 + 10 + 6 =
2. 12 + 16 =
3. 22 + 16 =
4. 32 + 16 =
5. 52 + 16 =
6. 18 − 10 − 6 =
7. 28 − 16 =
8. 38 − 16 =
9. ☐ − 16 = 42
10. ☐ + 16 = 68

C

1. Add 10 and 16.
2. Take 7 from 16.
3. The total of 3 and 16 is
4. The difference between 16 and 6 is
5. The sum of 16 and 9 is
6. 16 is 5 more than
7. Subtract 9 from 16.
8. 16 minus 8 is
9. 4 less than 16 is
10. 16 plus 6 is

Section 2   Test 7

A

1.  How many sticks?

2. 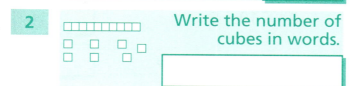 Write the number of cubes in words.

3. Draw beads on the abacus to show the number seventeen.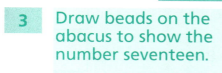

4. The total value of the coins is 17p. Which coin is missing? 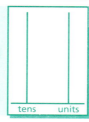 p

5. How much more do you need to make 20p?  p

6. You have ... You lose ...  How much have you got left? p

7. You have 17p. You buy 9p.  How much change do you get? p

8. You have ... You find ...  How much do you have now? p

9. Which month comes before April?

10. 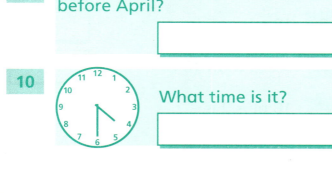 What time is it?

B

1. 4 + 10 + 7 =
2. 14 + 17 =
3. 24 + 17 =
4. 34 + 17 =
5. 54 + 17 =
6. 20 − 10 − 7 =
7. 30 − 17 =
8. 40 − 17 =
9. ☐ − 17 = 43
10. ☐ + 17 = 61

C

1. Add 7 and 17.
2. Take 5 from 17.
3. The total of 10 and 17 is
4. The difference between 17 and 6 is
5. The sum of 17 and 9 is
6. 17 is 7 more than
7. Subtract 9 from 17.
8. 17 minus 4 is
9. 8 less than 17 is
10. 17 plus 6 is

Section 2 Test 8

A — ANSWER

1.  How many sticks?

2.  Write the number of cubes in words.

3. Draw beads on the abacus to show the number eighteen.  tens units

4. The total value of the coins is 18p. Which coin is missing?  ? ___ p

5. How much more do you need to make 20p?  ___ p

6. You have  You spend How much have you got left? ___ p

7.  You have 18p. You buy 9p. How much change do you get? ___ p

8.  You have 10p 2p 1p 5p. You win 5p. How much do you have now? ___ p

9. Which month comes after November?

10.  What time is it?

B — ANSWER

1. 4 + 10 + 8 =
2. 4 + 10 + 10 − 2 =
3. 24 + 10 + 8 =
4. 24 + 10 + 10 − 2 =
5. 24 + 18 =
6. 20 − 10 − 8 =
7. 20 − 10 − 10 + 2 =
8. 20 − 18 =
9. ☐ − 18 = 42
10. ☐ + 18 = 42

C — ANSWER

1. Add 10 and 18.
2. Take 8 from 18.
3. The total of 8 and 18 is
4. The difference between 18 and 9 is
5. The sum of 18 and 4 is
6. 18 is 7 more than
7. Subtract 6 from 18.
8. 18 minus 5 is
9. 3 less than 18 is
10. 18 plus 2 is

26

Section 2   Test 9

A | ANSWER

1. 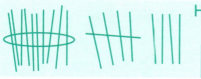 How many sticks?

2. 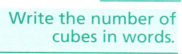 Write the number of cubes in words.

3. Draw beads on the abacus to show the number nineteen.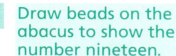

4. The total value of the coins is 19p. Which coin is missing? 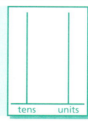 ___ p

5. How much more do you need to make 20p?   ___ p

6. You have You spend

   How much have you got left? ___ p

7. You have You buy
   How much change do you get? ___ p

8. You have 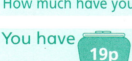 You find
   How much do you have now? ___ p

9. Which month comes after May?

10. What time is it?

B | ANSWER

1. 3 + 10 + 9 =
2. 3 + 10 + 10 − 1 =
3. 23 + 10 + 9 =
4. 23 + 10 + 10 − 1 =
5. 23 + 19 =
6. 40 − 10 − 9 =
7. 40 − 10 − 10 + 1 =
8. 40 − 19 =
9. ▉ − 19 = 41
10. ▉ + 19 = 42

C | ANSWER

1. Add 5 and 19.
2. Take 10 from 19.
3. The total of 4 and 19 is
4. The difference between 19 and 6 is
5. The sum of 19 and 9 is
6. 19 is 8 more than
7. Subtract 7 from 19.
8. 19 minus 4 is
9. 5 less than 19 is
10. 19 plus 3 is

Section 2 Test 10

A

1. Turn the picture into a sum.  ___ sets of ___

2. Turn the picture into a sum.  ___ sets of ___

3.  × 10 =

4. 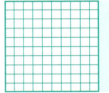 ÷ 10 =

5. How much altogether?  ___ p

6. × ■ = 70p

7. ÷ 10 = ___ p

8.  B is ten times as heavy as A. How heavy is B? ___ g

9. Which month comes after December?

10. What time is it?

B

1. 10, 20, 30, 40, ■
2. 10 + 10 + 10 =
3. 3 × 10 =
4. 10 + 10 + 10 + 10 + 10 =
5. 5 × 10 =
6. 90, 80, 70, 60, ■
7. 30 – 10 – 10 – 10 =
8. 30 ÷ 10 =
9. 70 ÷ 10 =
10. 90 ÷ 10 =

C

1. 8 sets of 10 are
2. How many tens in 70?
3. Four tens are
4. How many 10p coins make 50p?
5. 9 times 10 is
6. 6 multiplied by 10 is
7. 80 shared among 10 is
8. How many 10p coins are the same value as £1?
9. 60 divided by 10 is
10. How many wheels are there altogether on 10 bicycles?

Section 2 Test 11

A

1. 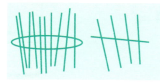 How many sticks?

2. Write the number of cubes in words.

3. Draw beads on the abacus to show the number seventeen.

4. The total value of the coins is 12p. Which coin is missing? 1p 5p 1p ? ___ p

5. How much more do you need to make 20p? 2p 2p 5p 2p 5p ___ p

6. You have 2p 2p 5p 5p You lose 10p. How much have you got left? ___ p

7. You have 18p You buy 7p cupcake. How much change do you get? ___ p

8. You have 2p 2p 2p 5p You find 10p. How much do you have now? ___ p

9. Which month comes after August?

10. What time is it?

B

1. 3 + 10 + 5 =
2. 23 + 15 =
3. 7 + 10 + 7 =
4. 47 + 17 =
5. 16 − 10 − 3 =
6. 56 − 13 =
7. 21 − 10 − 6 =
8. 31 − 16 =
9. ☐ − 19 = 4
10. ☐ + 19 = 24

C

1. Add 9 and 14.
2. Take 4 from 19.
3. The total of 12 and 3 is
4. The difference between 18 and 7 is
5. The sum of 11 and 2 is
6. 17 is 8 more than
7. Subtract 4 from 13.
8. 19 minus 6 is
9. 5 less than 10 is
10. 15 plus 5 is

29

Section 2 Test 12

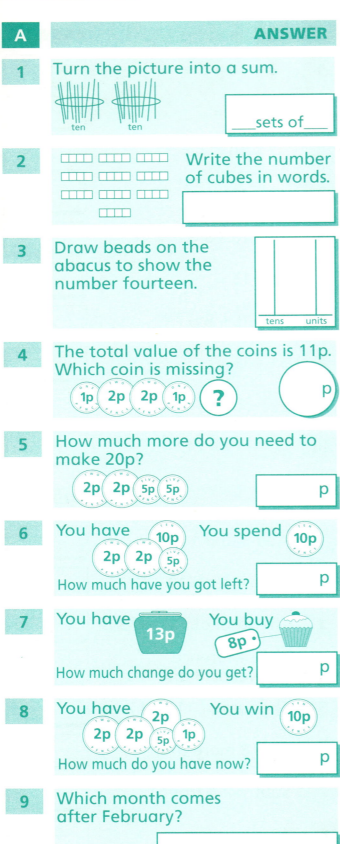

A

1. Turn the picture into a sum. ___ sets of ___
2. Write the number of cubes in words.
3. Draw beads on the abacus to show the number fourteen.
4. The total value of the coins is 11p. Which coin is missing? ___ p
5. How much more do you need to make 20p? ___ p
6. You have 10p, 2p, 2p, 5p. You spend 10p. How much have you got left? ___ p
7. You have 13p. You buy 8p. How much change do you get? ___ p
8. You have 2p, 2p, 2p, 5p, 1p. You win 10p. How much do you have now? ___ p
9. Which month comes after February?
10. What time is it?

B

1. 4 + 10 + 4 =
2. 44 + 14 =
3. 10 + 10 + 10 + 10 =
4. 4 × 10 =
5. 22 − 10 − 7 =
6. 32 − 17 =
7. 40 − 10 − 10 − 10 − 10 =
8. 40 ÷ 10 =
9. ☐ − 18 = 6
10. ☐ + 18 = 26

C

1. 5 sets of 10 are
2. How many tens are there in 60?
3. The total of 5 and 16 is
4. The difference between 13 and 7 is
5. 8 times 10 is
6. 11 is 8 more than
7. Subtract 9 from 14.
8. 40 divided by 10 is
9. 3 less than 18 is
10. 50 shared by 10 is

Section 3

Contents

TEST 1	Addition and subtraction of 20
TEST 2	Addition and subtraction of 30
TEST 3	Addition and subtraction of 40
TEST 4	Addition and subtraction of 50
TEST 5	Addition and subtraction of 60
TEST 6	Addition and subtraction of 70
TEST 7	Addition and subtraction of 80
TEST 8	Addition and subtraction of 90
TEST 9	Addition and subtraction of 100
TEST 10	Sets of 5
TEST 11	A mixture of tests 1 to 9 to test progress
TEST 12	A mixture of tests 1 to 10 to test progress

Date started:

Date finished:

Achievement Chart for Section 3
Colour the appropriate box for each question you got right

		1	2	3	4	5	6	7	8	9	10
Test 1	Part A										
	Part B										
	Part C										
Test 2	Part A										
	Part B										
	Part C										
Test 3	Part A										
	Part B										
	Part C										
Test 4	Part A										
	Part B										
	Part C										
Test 5	Part A										
	Part B										
	Part C										
Test 6	Part A										
	Part B										
	Part C										
Test 7	Part A										
	Part B										
	Part C										
Test 8	Part A										
	Part B										
	Part C										
Test 9	Part A										
	Part B										
	Part C										
Test 10	Part A										
	Part B										
	Part C										
Test 11	Part A										
	Part B										
	Part C										
Test 12	Part A										
	Part B										
	Part C										

Section 3   Test 1

A | ANSWER

1.  Write the number of sticks in words.

2. Draw beads on the abacus to show the number twenty.

3. 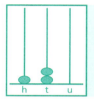 Write the number shown on the abacus.

4. How much more do you need to make £1? ___ p

5. How many 10p make 20p ?

6. How many  5p make  20p ?

7. How many 2p make  20p ?

8. What is the difference between
   A ———————— 20 cm
   and
   B ——————— 12 cm ? ___ cm

9. How many days are there in June? ___ days

10. What time is it?

B | ANSWER

1. 7 + 10 + 10 =
2. 17 + 2 tens =
3. 27 + 20 =
4. 37 + 20 =
5. 17, 37, 57, 77, ▢
6. 24 − 10 − 10 =
7. 24 − 2 tens =
8. 34 − 20 =
9. 44 − 20 =
10. 84, 64, 44, ▢, 4

C | ANSWER

1. Add 7p and 20p. ___ p
2. Take 5p from 20p. ___ p
3. The total cost of 20p and 9p is ___ p
4. The difference in price between 7p and 20p is ___ p
5. The sum of 6p and 20p is ___ p
6. 20p is 8p more than ___ p
7. If you spend 10p, your change from 20p is ___ p
8. If you have 20p and you lose 4p, you will be left with ___ p
9. 3p less than 20p is ___ p
10. 12p plus 20p is ___ p

Section 3 Test 2

A | ANSWER

1. Write the number of sticks in words.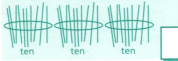

2. Draw beads on the abacus to show the number thirty.

3. 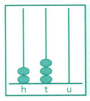 Write the number shown on the abacus.

4. How much more do you need to make £1? ___ p

5. How many 10p make 10p 20p ?

6. How many 5p make 10p 20p ?

7. How many 2p make 10p 20p ?

8. What is the difference in mass between A and B?  ___ g
   B = 20 g   A = 30 g

9. How many days are there in April? ___ days

10.  What time is it?

B | ANSWER

1. 6 + 10 + 10 + 10 =
2. 16 + 3 tens =
3. 26 + 30 =
4. 36 + 30 =
5. 6, 36, 66, ☐, 126
6. 32 – 10 – 10 – 10 =
7. 42 – 3 tens =
8. 52 – 30 =
9. 62 – 30 =
10. 122, 92, 62, 32, ☐

C | ANSWER

1. Add 7 cm and 30 cm. ___ cm
2. Take 5 cm from 30 cm. ___ cm
3. The total length of 30 cm and 19 cm is ___ cm
4. The difference between 7 cm and 30 cm is ___ cm
5. The sum of 16 cm and 30 cm is ___ cm
6. 30 cm is 8 cm longer than ___ cm
7. Subtract 11 cm from 30 cm. ___ cm
8. 30 cm minus 14 cm is ___ cm
9. 13 cm shorter than 30 cm is ___ cm
10. 20 cm plus 30 cm is ___ cm

Section 3 Test 3

A

1. Write the number of sticks in words. [four tens of sticks shown]

2. Draw beads on the abacus to show the number forty.

3. Write the number shown on the abacus.

4. How much more do you need to make £1? [20p, 20p] ___ p

5. How many 10p make 20p 20p ?

6. How many 5p make 20p 20p ?

7. How many 2p make 20p 20p ?

8. What is the difference between 20p 20p and 10p ? ___ p

9. How many days are there in September? ___ days

10. What time is it?

B

1. 5 + 10 + 10 + 10 + 10 =
2. 15 + 4 tens =
3. 25 + 40 =
4. 35 + 40 =
5. 5, 45, 85, 125, ▨
6. 41 − 10 − 10 − 10 − 10 =
7. 51 − 4 tens =
8. 61 − 40 =
9. 71 − 40 =
10. 201, 161, 121, 81, ▨

C

1. Add 7 kg and 40 kg. ___ kg
2. Take 5 kg from 40 kg. ___ kg
3. The total mass of 40 kg and 20 kg is ___ kg
4. The difference between 30 kg and 40 kg is ___ kg
5. The sum of 16 kg and 40 kg is ___ kg
6. 40 kg is 8 kg heavier than ___ kg
7. Subtract 11 kg from 40 kg. ___ kg
8. 40 kg minus 4 kg is ___ kg
9. 10 kg lighter than 40 kg is ___ kg
10. 12 kg plus 40 kg is ___ kg

Section 3 Test 4

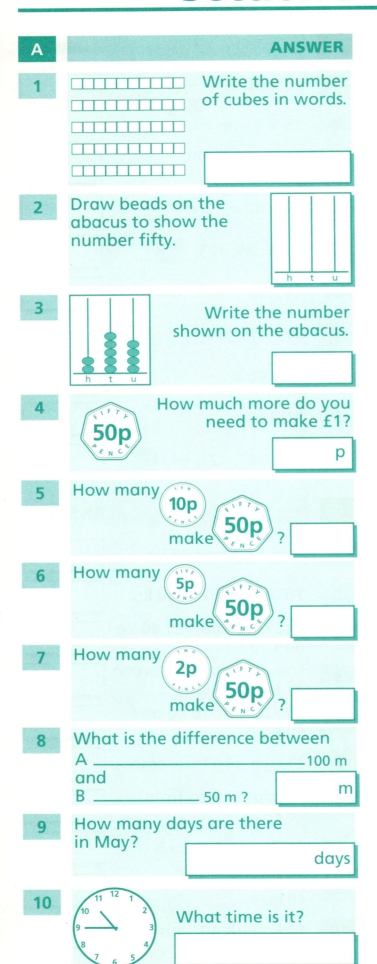

A

1. Write the number of cubes in words.
2. Draw beads on the abacus to show the number fifty.
3. Write the number shown on the abacus.
4. How much more do you need to make £1? ____ p
5. How many 10p make 50p?
6. How many 5p make 50p?
7. How many 2p make 50p?
8. What is the difference between A _____ 100 m and B _____ 50 m? ____ m
9. How many days are there in May? ____ days
10. What time is it?

B

1. 5 + 5 tens =
2. 15 + 5 tens =
3. 25 + 50 =
4. 35 + 50 =
5. 5, 55, 105, 155, ▢
6. 59 − 5 tens =
7. 69 − 5 tens =
8. 79 − 50 =
9. 89 − 50 =
10. 259, 209, 159, 109, ▢

C

1. Add £30 and £50.
2. Take £5 from £50.
3. The total value of £50 and £40 is
4. The difference between £20 and £50 is
5. The sum of £16 and £50 is
6. £50 is £8 more than
7. If you spend £15, what is your change from £50?
8. £50 minus £40 is
9. You have £50. You spend £10. How much have you left?
10. £19 plus £50 is

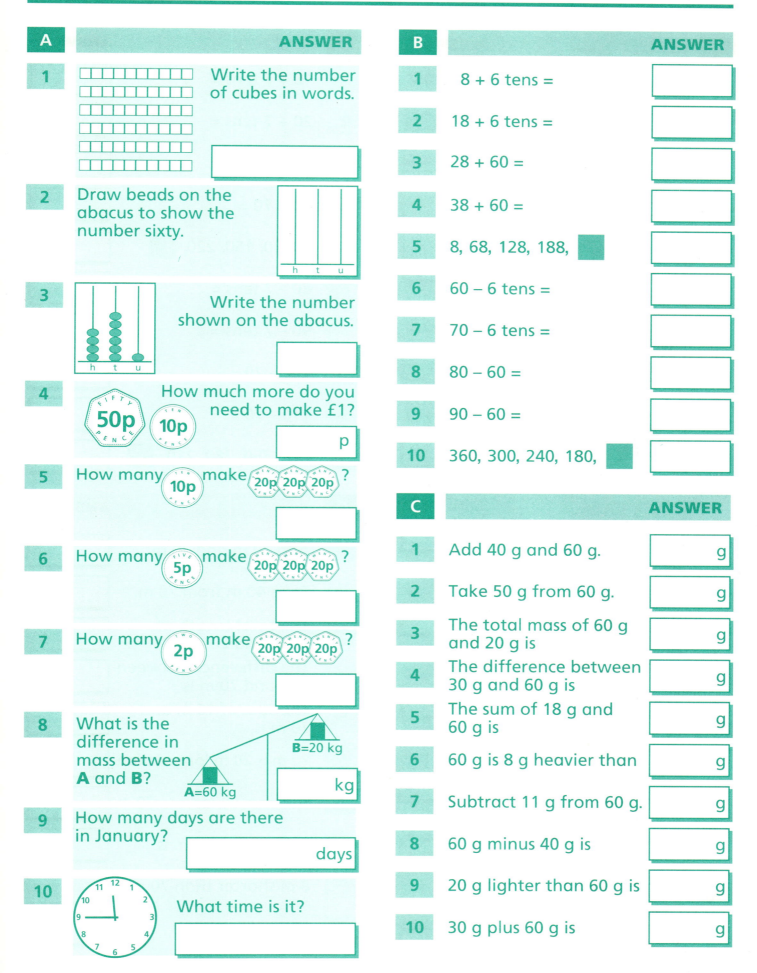

Section 3 Test 6

A | ANSWER

1.  Write the number of cubes in words.

2. Draw beads on the abacus to show the number seventy.

3. 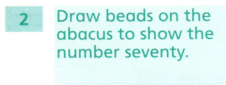 Write the number shown on the abacus.

4.  How much more do you need to make £1? ___ p

5.  How many 10p make 50p 20p?

6.  How many 5p make 50p 20p?

7.  How many 2p make 50p 20p?

8. What is the difference between  50p 20p and 10p 10p 10p? ___ p

9. How many days are there in October? ___ days

10.  What time is it?

B | ANSWER

1. 10 + 7 tens =
2. 20 + 7 tens =
3. 30 + 70 =
4. 40 + 70 =
5. 10, 80, 150, 220, ▩
6. 80 – 7 tens =
7. 90 – 7 tens =
8. 100 – 70 =
9. 110 – 70 =
10. 420, 350, 280, 210, ▩

C | ANSWER

1. Add 30 m and 70 m. ___ m
2. Take 40 m from 70 m. ___ m
3. The total length of 70 m and 20 m is ___ m
4. The difference between 7 m and 70 m is ___ m
5. The sum of 16 m and 70 m is ___ m
6. 70 m is 20 m longer than ___ m
7. Subtract 50 m from 70 m. ___ m
8. 70 m minus 60 m is ___ m
9. 8 m shorter than 70 m is ___ m
10. 19 m plus 70 m is ___ m

38

Section 3 Test 7

A | ANSWER

1.  Write the number of cubes in words.

2. Draw beads on the abacus to show the number eighty.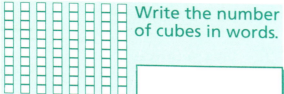

3. 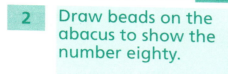 Write the number shown on the abacus.

4. 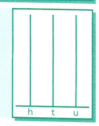 How much more do you need to make £1? ____ p

5. How many 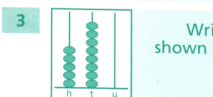 make  ?

6. How many  make ?

7. How many  make ?

8. What is the difference between  and ? ____ litres

9. How many days are there in July? ____ days

10.  What time is it?

B | ANSWER

1. 10 + 8 tens =
2. 20 + 8 tens =
3. 30 + 80 =
4. 40 + 80 =
5. 0, 80, 160, 240, ▣
6. 80 − 8 tens =
7. 90 − 8 tens =
8. 100 − 80 =
9. 110 − 80 =
10. 480, 400, 320, 240, ▣

C | ANSWER

1. Add 19 m and 80 m. ____ m
2. Take 60 m from 80 m. ____ m
3. The total length of 80 m and 15 m is ____ m
4. The difference between 70 m and 80 m is ____ m
5. The sum of 6 m and 80 m is ____ m
6. 80 m is 30 m longer than ____ m
7. Subtract 20 m from 80 m. ____ m
8. 80 m minus 40 m is ____ m
9. 30 m less than 80 m is ____ m
10. 8 m plus 80 m is ____ m

39

Section 3 Test 8

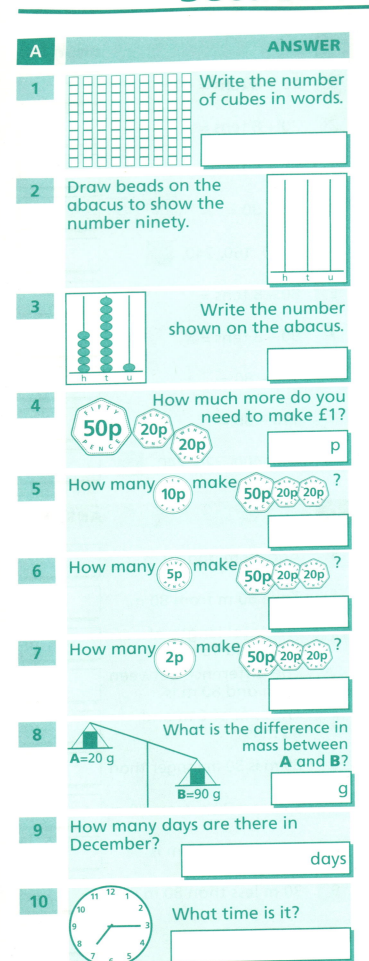

A

1. Write the number of cubes in words.
2. Draw beads on the abacus to show the number ninety.
3. Write the number shown on the abacus.
4. How much more do you need to make £1? ___ p
5. How many 10p make 50p 20p 20p?
6. How many 5p make 50p 20p 20p?
7. How many 2p make 50p 20p 20p?
8. What is the difference in mass between A and B? A=20 g, B=90 g ___ g
9. How many days are there in December? ___ days
10. What time is it?

B

1. 10 + 9 tens =
2. 20 + 9 tens =
3. 30 + 90 =
4. 40 + 90 =
5. 0, 90, 180, 270, ▇
6. 100 − 9 tens =
7. 110 − 9 tens =
8. 120 − 90 =
9. 130 − 90 =
10. 540, 450, 360, 270, ▇

C

1. Add 9 min and 90 min. ___ min
2. Take 50 min from 90 min. ___ min
3. The total time taken for two TV programmes lasting 90 min and 20 min is ___ min
4. The difference between 60 min and 90 min is ___ min
5. The sum of 6 min and 90 min is ___ min
6. 90 min is 5 min longer than ___ min
7. Subtract 15 min from 90 min. ___ min
8. 90 min minus 40 min is ___ min
9. 30 min less than 90 min is ___ min
10. 8 min plus 90 min is ___ min

Section 3 Test 9

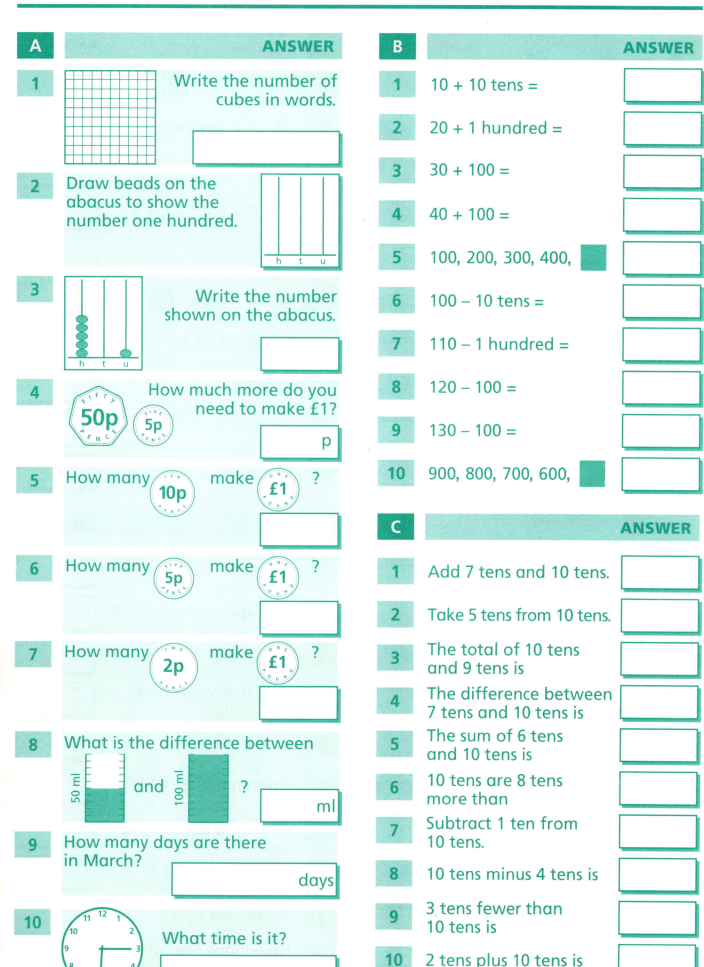

Section 3 Test 10

A		ANSWER
1	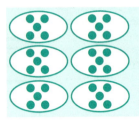 Turn the picture into a sum.	___ sets of ___
2	Turn the picture into a sum. 	___ sets of ___
3	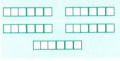 × 5 =	
4	 ÷ 5 =	
5	How much altogether? 	p
6	 5p × ☐ = 40p	
7	 20p ÷ 5 =	p
8	B is five times as heavy as A. How heavy is B? A = 9 g	g
9	How many days are there in August?	days
10	What time is it?	

B		ANSWER
1	5, 10, 15, 20, ☐	
2	5 + 5 + 5 + 5 =	
3	4 × 5 =	
4	5 + 5 + 5 + 5 + 5 + 5 =	
5	6 × 5 =	
6	50, 45, 40, 35, ☐	
7	15 − 5 − 5 − 5 =	
8	15 ÷ 5 =	
9	35 ÷ 5 =	
10	40 ÷ 5 =	

C		ANSWER
1	8 sets of 5 are	
2	How many fives in 30?	
3	9 fives are	
4	How many 5p coins make 50p?	
5	7 times 5 is	
6	6 multiplied by 5 is	
7	40 shared among 5 is	
8	If I change 20p into 5p coins, how many will I get?	
9	45 divided by 5 is	
10	How many toes are there on 10 feet?	

Section 3   Test 11

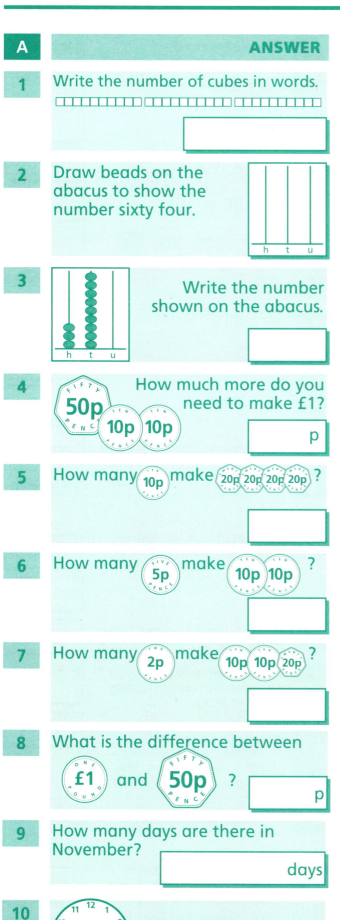

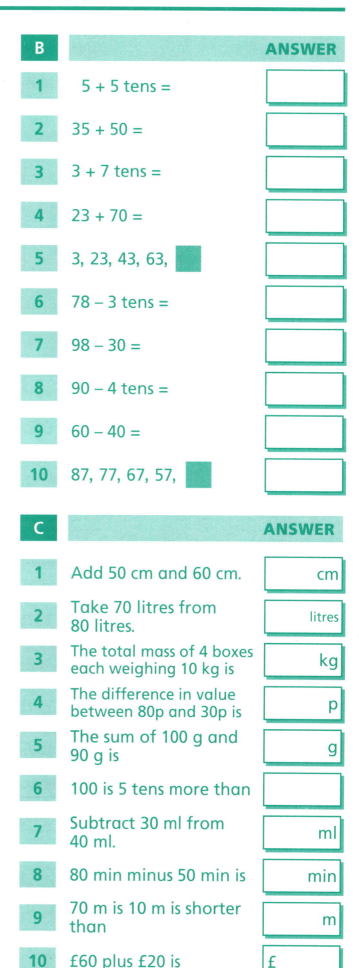

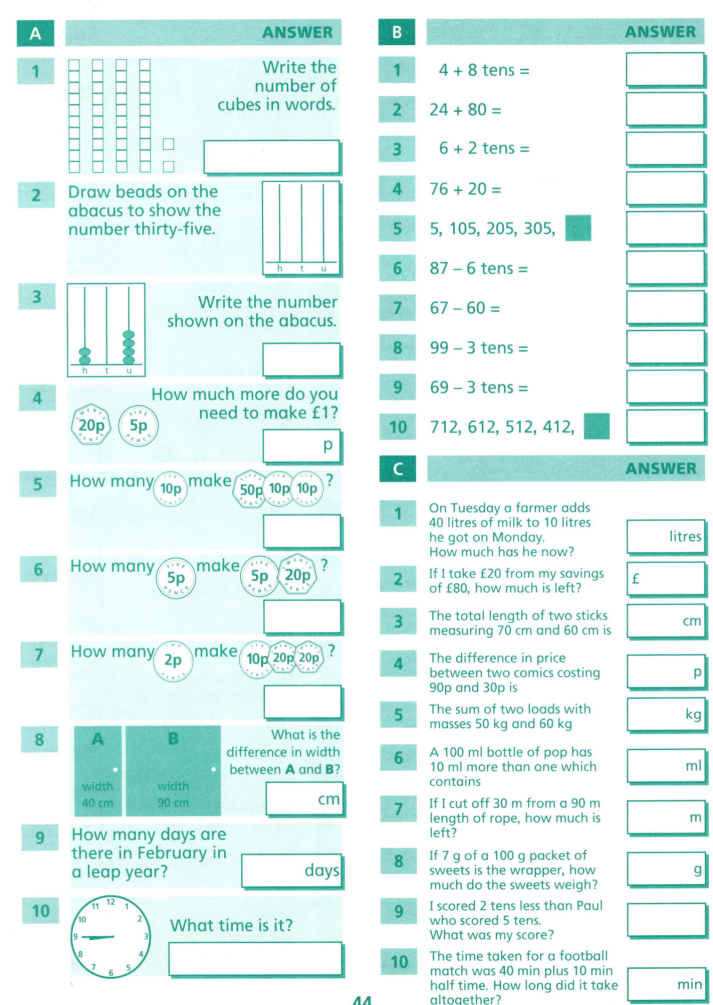

Just Facts

DOUBLES

1 + 1 = ☐	2 − 1 = ☐
2 + 2 = ☐	4 − 2 = ☐
3 + 3 = ☐	6 − 3 = ☐
4 + 4 = ☐	8 − 4 = ☐
5 + 5 = ☐	10 − 5 = ☐
6 + 6 = ☐	12 − 6 = ☐
7 + 7 = ☐	14 − 7 = ☐
8 + 8 = ☐	16 − 8 = ☐
9 + 9 = ☐	18 − 9 = ☐
10 + 10 = ☐	20 − 10 = ☐

NEAR DOUBLES

1 + 2 = ☐	2 + 1 = ☐	3 − 1 = ☐	3 − 2 = ☐
2 + 3 = ☐	3 + 2 = ☐	5 − 2 = ☐	5 − 3 = ☐
3 + 4 = ☐	4 + 3 = ☐	7 − 3 = ☐	7 − 4 = ☐
4 + 5 = ☐	5 + 4 = ☐	9 − 4 = ☐	9 − 5 = ☐
5 + 6 = ☐	6 + 5 = ☐	11 − 5 = ☐	11 − 6 = ☐
6 + 7 = ☐	7 + 6 = ☐	13 − 6 = ☐	13 − 7 = ☐
7 + 8 = ☐	8 + 7 = ☐	15 − 7 = ☐	15 − 8 = ☐
8 + 9 = ☐	9 + 8 = ☐	17 − 8 = ☐	17 − 9 = ☐

NEAR NEAR DOUBLES

1 + 3 = ☐	3 + 1 = ☐	4 − 1 = ☐	4 − 3 = ☐
2 + 4 = ☐	4 + 2 = ☐	6 − 2 = ☐	6 − 4 = ☐
3 + 5 = ☐	5 + 3 = ☐	8 − 3 = ☐	8 − 5 = ☐
4 + 6 = ☐	6 + 4 = ☐	10 − 4 = ☐	10 − 6 = ☐
5 + 7 = ☐	7 + 5 = ☐	12 − 5 = ☐	12 − 7 = ☐
6 + 8 = ☐	8 + 6 = ☐	14 − 6 = ☐	14 − 8 = ☐
7 + 9 = ☐	9 + 7 = ☐	16 − 7 = ☐	16 − 9 = ☐
8 + 10 = ☐	10 + 8 = ☐	18 − 8 = ☐	18 − 10 = ☐

Just Facts

COUNTING ON 1 and related facts

1 + 1 =	1 + 1 =	2 − 1 =	2 − 1 =
2 + 1 =	1 + 2 =	3 − 1 =	3 − 2 =
3 + 1 =	1 + 3 =	4 − 1 =	4 − 3 =
4 + 1 =	1 + 4 =	5 − 1 =	5 − 4 =
5 + 1 =	1 + 5 =	6 − 1 =	6 − 5 =
6 + 1 =	1 + 6 =	7 − 1 =	7 − 6 =
7 + 1 =	1 + 7 =	8 − 1 =	8 − 7 =
8 + 1 =	1 + 8 =	9 − 1 =	9 − 8 =
9 + 1 =	1 + 9 =	10 − 1 =	10 − 9 =

COUNTING ON 2 and related facts

1 + 2 =	2 + 1 =	3 − 2 =	3 − 1 =
2 + 2 =	2 + 2 =	4 − 2 =	4 − 2 =
3 + 2 =	2 + 3 =	5 − 2 =	5 − 3 =
4 + 2 =	2 + 4 =	6 − 2 =	6 − 4 =
5 + 2 =	2 + 5 =	7 − 2 =	7 − 5 =
6 + 2 =	2 + 6 =	8 − 2 =	8 − 6 =
7 + 2 =	2 + 7 =	9 − 2 =	9 − 7 =
8 + 2 =	2 + 8 =	10 − 2 =	10 − 8 =
9 + 2 =	2 + 9 =	11 − 2 =	11 − 9 =

ADDING 10 and related facts

1 + 10 =	10 + 1 =	11 − 10 =	11 − 1 =
2 + 10 =	10 + 2 =	12 − 10 =	12 − 2 =
3 + 10 =	10 + 3 =	13 − 10 =	13 − 3 =
4 + 10 =	10 + 4 =	14 − 10 =	14 − 4 =
5 + 10 =	10 + 5 =	15 − 10 =	15 − 5 =
6 + 10 =	10 + 6 =	16 − 10 =	16 − 6 =
7 + 10 =	10 + 7 =	17 − 10 =	17 − 7 =
8 + 10 =	10 + 8 =	18 − 10 =	18 − 8 =
9 + 10 =	10 + 9 =	19 − 10 =	19 − 9 =

Just Facts

MAKING 10 and related facts

1 + 9 =	9 + 1 =	10 − 1 =	10 − 9 =
2 + 8 =	8 + 2 =	10 − 2 =	10 − 8 =
3 + 7 =	7 + 3 =	10 − 3 =	10 − 7 =
4 + 6 =	6 + 4 =	10 − 4 =	10 − 6 =
5 + 5 =	5 + 5 =	10 − 5 =	10 − 5 =

ADDING 9 and related facts

1 + 9 =	9 + 1 =	10 − 9 =	10 − 1 =
2 + 9 =	9 + 2 =	11 − 9 =	11 − 2 =
3 + 9 =	9 + 3 =	12 − 9 =	12 − 3 =
4 + 9 =	9 + 4 =	13 − 9 =	13 − 4 =
5 + 9 =	9 + 5 =	14 − 9 =	14 − 5 =
6 + 9 =	9 + 6 =	15 − 9 =	15 − 6 =
7 + 9 =	9 + 7 =	16 − 9 =	16 − 7 =
8 + 9 =	9 + 8 =	17 − 9 =	17 − 8 =
9 + 9 =	9 + 9 =	18 − 9 =	18 − 9 =

ADDING 8 and related facts

1 + 8 =	8 + 1 =	9 − 8 =	9 − 1 =
2 + 8 =	8 + 2 =	10 − 8 =	10 − 2 =
3 + 8 =	8 + 3 =	11 − 8 =	11 − 3 =
4 + 8 =	8 + 4 =	12 − 8 =	12 − 4 =
5 + 8 =	8 + 5 =	13 − 8 =	13 − 5 =
6 + 8 =	8 + 6 =	14 − 8 =	14 − 6 =
7 + 8 =	8 + 7 =	15 − 8 =	15 − 7 =
8 + 8 =	8 + 8 =	16 − 8 =	16 − 8 =
9 + 8 =	8 + 9 =	17 − 8 =	17 − 9 =

Workbooks published by Schofield & Sims Ltd

EARLY WRITING			
Early Writing	Books 1-4	Age range	5-8

ENGLISH			
Basic Skills	Books 1-5	Age range	6-8
Guide Lines	Books 1-5	Age range	6-8
Springboard	Books 1-8	Age range	7-11

MENTAL ARITHMETIC			
Mental Arithmetic	Introductory Book Books 1-5	Age range	6-12

NUMBER			
Number Books	Books 1-5	Age range	5-7

PHONICS			
Sound Practice	Books 1-5	Age range	6-8

SCIENCE			
Starting Science	Books 1-3	Age range	6-8

SPELLING			
Early Spellings	Books 1-3	Age range	6-8
Spellaway	Books 1-3	Age range	8-12

Schofield & Sims Ltd Huddersfield

ISBN 0-7217-2446-9